COLUMNATED RUINS

A Collection of Poems

Corydon J. Doyle

2011

CONTENTS

COLUMNATED RUINS

For Carolyn,
my muse

WESTHAMPTON

The House on Church Lane

I love these walls,
    the feels,
       the sounds.

My house stands atop the world
under a cascading sky.
    Where my imaginary
    reality
    will always exist
regardless of who claims it.

The price of my memories
is too much for you,
and this was a place
that was never empty.

Winter

Though dark and gray
the skies appear,
an unbound mind
this time of year.

My garden sits
beneath the shade
of neighbor's trees,
a winter's glade.

I revel in
the falling snow
like water games,
a fountain's flow.

These days of mine
are his and hers
to ponder on
what dream occurs.

Returning home
from winter broods
I see the lights
in yuletide mood.

I think of nights
in moments wake,
beautiful child
in white snowflakes.

Alone again
in white repose,
I'll walk again
this path I chose.

Spring

Beneath my carved tree,
enjoying the new shade,
is my mother's dear mother
awake like no other.

> She embraces the nape
> of this season's earth,
> and spreads out beyond
> my world to abscond.

With daylight's stitch
she dresses the green
for the love she bestows
under a violet halo.

> Show me the spring
> in remembrance of days
> when I woke under skies
> free of any disguise.

The few weeks you're here,
before the tides change,
I'll bring one back home
and to places I'll roam.

> In my garden you'll grow
> where my children will know
> of me, your grandson
> and our days in the sun.

Summer

At my side, in my hand
a young girl sings softly
for herself to hear.

The music,
      the crowds,
            the hand of her cousin,

These are the things that keep her safe
      from her own inhibitions.

The music and laughter
resonate
with the days lingering heat.

In her eyes, the world is as unfamiliar
as the strangers I see around us.
But together we remind ourselves
of all things innocent,
      and I think to myself,

which one of us is holding the other?

Autumn

This time of year,
to me,
is always in the past.
And you are there
poised amidst
the reverently weeping trees
that are my memories.
You're smiling at me
and whispering words
I forgot.
But you are there.
I can see us
in autumns that will be.
You,
and I,
and another.
She will share
our everything –
our love
as endless
as the autumn
my mind keeps bringing.

The Open Book

A Children's Tale

There's a store with a door
that's redder than red.
 And inside this store,
 stacked tall on the floor,
 are books upon books
 like standing chess rooks.
 And among these fine stacks,
and the shelves and the racks,
 are kids and a cat
 making dusty cat tracks.

It's cozy and warm
 where friendly crowds swarm
 to laugh and converse
 with novels and verse.
 Where coffee and smiles
 walk through the aisles
 and music and arts
 rise when the day starts.
 It's a place just for you
 and friends, family too,
 for there's always a read
 to follow your lead.
 A corner awaits
 when you walk through the
gates,
 but this poet resides
 on the classical side…

There's a story for you,
 fictitious or true,
 that will open your eyes
 to wisdom and lies.
 And once it is read

pictures dance in your head
 of epics once told
 and legends of old,
 of fortunes revealed
 and broken hearts healed
from days in the sun
to nights just begun.

So if you get lost
 from life's truant cost
 just follow the cat
 making dusty cat tracks
 to the boy with balloons
 skipping under the moon
 from the store with the door
 that is redder than red
 where inside the store
 stacked tall on the floor
 are books upon books
like standing chess rooks
 where the queen of the scene
 and her band of bright teens
 will read you a page
 from the mind or the stage
 to show you anew
 the sky bright and blue.
 Then you'll truly be lost
 through the sun and the frost
and you won't want to leave
 nor grovel nor grieve;

For you've found it at last
the one place to look
through your future and past
your own Open Book.

The Gazebo

On these pensive afternoons,
before twilight,
I gather my effects
and return to the gazebo.
My open sanctuary stands
among the echoes of children's
summer
where I bask in the fragrance
of an evergreen dawn.

I read of a king,
bereft of his daughters,
and lose myself in the wine
and Sir William's words.
Until I recall
my life under the weather
vane,
I'll stay hidden
in the hallways of verse.

The Bakery

Upon entering, I see
that this place is black
and white –

    The table where
    I so often stare down
    at defeat…

        The glass encasements
        where children beg
        and plead…

            The intentions in the corner
            sitting passively
            for now…

                The lord of the manor
                stalking the grounds,
                grinning…

                    And here am I
                    the modern dualist,
                    failing…

The Magic Triangle

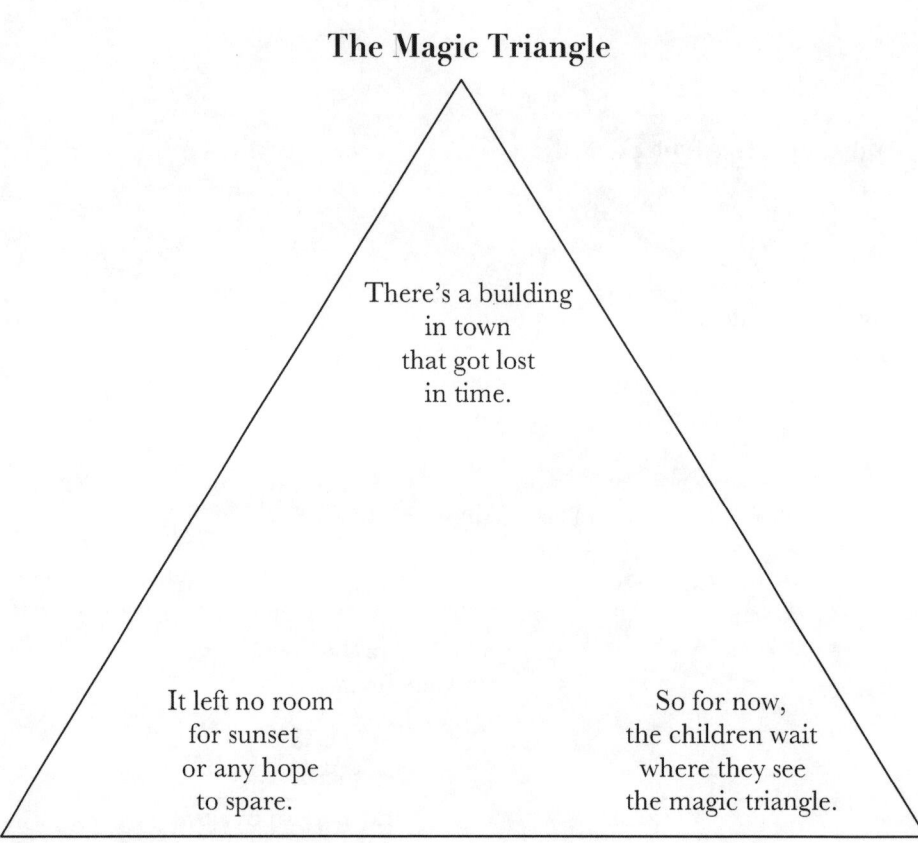

There's a building
in town
that got lost
in time.

It left no room
for sunset
or any hope
to spare.

So for now,
the children wait
where they see
the magic triangle.

Lady Duerschmidt

Above my bed
hangs
a Duerschmidt
depicting
a bridge.

This bridge is
my summer.
This bridge is
my father.
This bridge is
my memory.
This bridge is
my unknown.

How nice it feels
to lose one's self
on a canvas
of reality.

Does anyone know
this bridge
I feel?

Lady Duerschmidt knows.

Of Sapling's Bough

This was a place
I used to wander
on aimless nights
with thoughts to ponder.
But now I find
I'm sinking here
through strict repose
each flagrant year.

This world's visage
is but a shade
of sapling's bough
time shan't evade.
The ones who stalk
the doors deceased
feel as I do,
I hope at least.

The anguished walls
I knew so well
are lost unto
consumer hell.
Yet still I see
a younger mind
who'll march these halls
with fears resigned.

I see it clear,
the truth in you,
a simple maze
a grand haiku.

Each season will pass
as we drift freely along
this place called Main Street.

QUOGUE

The House on Ogden Pond

I fell asleep
one autumn night
and woke to see,
with sweet delight,
my Ogden Pond
bathed in sunlight
and set behind
two birds in flight.

Above the tides,
from ocean's sway,
the poets glide
like avis rays.
One's wings as white
as winter's day,
the other's black
as dusk's decay.

The glass remains
beneath their trace
of gentle words
in hunter's grace.
Their song is sung
in sea's embrace
to wait no more
and leave this place.

The morning's come
from distant wings
and paints through dawn
my sufferings.
The rafters high
I'll try to cling
and fear each day
approaching spring.

Winter

I am alive
in the hometown of my father,
and I feel as reclusive as
his memories of himself.

The beaches here
do not belong to me.
They belong to no one.
People dismiss these truths.
It is an idea as fleeting
as the warmth in our breath
we need to abandon.
It is an idea as fleeting
as the sands to which
they try to cling.

We belong to the beach,

yet we betray it.

I walk the dunes
in summer's eve
and summer's wake
to counsel the waves
that cry in bereavement
of its abandonment.
And it will know
of winters possessed
by a figure not following
but strengthening the footsteps
of his father
walking towards a horizon
of nowhere near.

Spring

The road up ahead is going to bend
and I will be saluted by my arching elders,
who blossom year after year
in honor of some forgotten soothsayer who,
with hands in the earth,
somehow knew of these days when I,
      returning from my misgivings,
would reach this bend in the road
and feel the embrace of the concrete,
and see,
      with eyes shut,
the curve outside reason
as it cradles my familiar body
with the warm tones of a grandfather who,
      like this path,
is free to remember things,
but leaves you to see the world
as is.

Summer

I need to find what's left of this world,
where the trees can steady
their tiring gestures
and help me escape the heat.
My body has become a devout metronome.
The heat
dilutes my senses,
my very being,
like the shadow of the tide
being dragged out from the shore,

or,

I can leave this body;
Move as pure thought,
an enigma burying itself
through a haze of the illuminated world
to find secure darkness.
Here my strides will quicken
and the air's blasphemous texture
will weaken and crumble
like dust upon my beating heart.
I can step out from my frail façade
to exist among the unobserved
and move like a musical epilogue
from a deafening silence.
To be
is to know one's self
as is,
and I am the black spot
moving across the sun
in defiance
of its staggering relevance.

Autumn

I futilely ignore it twice in a
day.
It sits just past the edge of the
grass
like a child
hiding their face in their knees
muffling the sobs
I can't help but hear.

It's not nostalgia
when I think of what
happened.
    The brutality of the storm…

It's not a nightmare either,
because there is no comfort
here
of waking to compose
my thoughts
on some ignorance of reality.

No,
I live that old violence
everyday.

Each time I see it,
I hear that last haunting
breath
I took before it began.
I'm cursed with responsibility
to keep my eyes open,
though I'd like no other
escape.
Instead, I see it all.

The first strike is revolting.
How much easier

this would be
if you had lived past
your bearing
to rid you of your resolve,
that I know you would
understand.

I refuse to think elsewhere,
just awaiting the moment
when my only relief comes
from leaving the axe
by your remains
to rust in the oncoming rain
which is all it deserves.

I could not burn you;
to bask in your deathly
potential
like some demon.
All that's left
is to try not to look
at the last pieces
of where your body broke
from where you grew
for however many years
before my arrival.

And each time I pass,
my hopeless empathy
brings back that moment
when I stood over you
and what it must have
been like for you
to have this boy
free you from this cruel realm.

White Deer

A friend told me once
they're afraid of missing things,
not afraid to die.

But how can I live
with infinite transcendence
removed from my fears?

In my helpless thirst
I'm faced with unknown questions
poisoned with terror.

Quench naivety,
swallowing the rhetoric
my youth may betray.

And in that moment
I fear I'll choke on all things
unpredictable.

The white deer appears,
the lone figure of my qualms,
and it frightens me.

A black swan occurs
and I weigh its origins
and what it intends.

I leave in silence
fears of inexperience
which guide everyone.

The Woman with No Name

She stood at the edge
of an abyss of chance.
And for that,
I am the coward.
For it was not the first time
we crossed paths,
but the first time one of us
stepped off.
I can not identify what it was
that she evolved to
in the moment –
the same thing
that I still lack.

It is because of this
that she is undoubtedly someone
just not for me to know.

Anonymity's strength
is like the deceptiveness of glass,
and as vulnerable
in the midst of a hurricane;
one which will converge
each morning we pass
in the translation of our brief nods.

The Lion on the Swing

One day I saw a girl
      who discovered it all.
            For the shortest of moments
                  I wish she'd catch my eye
                        to clue me into her life
                              and teach me things that matter.

                              I know who she is
                        because we live in a place
                  that elegantly constricts the population
            in a manner unknown to the poor,
      which only checker piece kings
            can truly appreciate.

But this queen stands alone
      roaring in ferocious glee
            for the heavens to hear;
                  the lion on the swing
                        with the world lassoed on the ropes
                              I hope she'll never release.

                              Forever after that,
                              I envy her life then,
                  realizing truth after truth
            in each pendulum movement
      that brings her genius closer
and ticks my life away.

The White Horse

Everyone knows the creature
poised against time.
It has stood there
forever
staring into something
that none of us can see.
      That is why we are afraid of it.
      That is why tales of its destruction
      were carried quickly.
      That is why we rebuilt
      with tears in our eyes.
We all love and fear
the white horse.
      We love it for its tenacity,
      which does not seem unnatural
      for a figure of stone.
We fear it for the emotions
it antagonizes in young hearts.
Have you looked at
its plaintive smile?
It will leave its intentions unknown
forever
until the next bold youth
reacts in an existential whim –
a budding Raskolnikov
prepared to bludgeon his hopes
to achieve the sights
only the white horse
sees.
      If it happens again,
      when it happens again,
      I hope he remembers
      to take a piece
      to add to his
      columnnated ruins.

Empty Grandfather

Within this small town,
on a frequented street,
on an abused property,
in a forgotten house
inside an abandoned room
in the mind of the man
rings two grandfather clocks.

One echoes the times he's wasted,
one chimes the time he can redeem.
The choice is his alone.
Yet with each fading tone
more dust settles
in the grooves of his brain.
He lives in a universe
of monotonic chimes.
All he knows,
all he clings to,
is that one chime,
soon to come,
will be a requiem
that no one will sing.

The windows are smudged
in and of that forgotten house.
On the inside
his tears can wipe them clean
leaving him to see time's mess.
That is what he does not know.

If you get close enough
to peer inside
you
will have to wipe away the time
that has grown outside.
That is what you do not know.

Bridges
Haiku

Burning the bridges
will not halt the dynasty
beyond confusion.

THE BEACH

The House on the Dunes

There's a house on the dunes
that scares the shit out of me.
It's filled will all the dark things
the imagination of a child
can conjure.
I see my father's face
staring at the road ahead
coming from some place
forgotten,
but the same every time.
His voice in the tale
stretches like a trap
in the dark
waiting to snap.

Then,
it is struck by the headlights
at the climax,
refusing to be forced back
by my heaving chest.
It's so small,
so impossibly small,
to fill with the horror
the tale tells to have transpired.
I get only one brief moment
for my brothers,
who can not look,
to face that house
and this time
hopefully see
a smile through a window,
a light on,
a new garden.

But nothing…

Winter

The sons and daughters of the beach
love it all year long.
Those who would embrace it
against the cold
who would face the waters
in hope of being accepted
only to replenish
the salt water in their veins,
the sand in their skin,
and the sun in their eyes.

Spring

They are devoured
by the compelling notion
of love.
These…
children
who stand
hand in hand
yet alone,
stowing themselves away
underneath the warmth
of their hearts
that they know,
they know,
is deceiving them.
The wisdom of youth
comes clad in indecisiveness,
wreaking of sex
with a devotion
almost masochistic.
I,
we all,
were them once.
And like them
I broke to pieces.
It had to happen.
Because today
when the next child
builds their castle
I think
We're in there somewhere.

Summer

I.

The world outside our salty fire
is empty,
except for the sound of the waves,
and this is a time
that is only remembered
in the embers
that will burn even after
the funeral we give it each time
before stepping into sand
bereft of its once epic reach.
Like each night before
we walk back
through the emptiness
with renewed hope for the world.

II.

She straddles the line
that keeps me in the present
against the moon
soothing the ocean
leaving me close enough to kiss
her shadow
that seems to reach
the whole damn world.

Autumn
Haiku

Blanket of crimson,
the young heron scribes wisdom
of sweet loveliness.

Dune Road

When the world
is thirteen miles long
I'll explore a jetty
and be welcomed as a hero.

But until then,
I'll scream my head off
towards that wild blue
to see how far
my strength can take me
towards the edge of the map.
I'll take my soul
and skip it like stones
thrown by children
who haven't seen the horizons yet.

Those Gradient Peaks

I can't capture
the one straight line
that doesn't really exist
but is too much for me to see.
The breath that ignore me
    and surround me,
the spit that condemn me
    and embrace me,
the arms that strangle me
    and arrange me,

All curved.   It is a love
        that is as barren
      as my mind makes it
         because,
       what the hell,
     that's just our fault.

        I can create an
          Oasis,
           sure,
         but why?

Why? *we ask…* Because those gradient peaks
          sacrifice themselves
            year after year

              after year

and we look towards the one straight line
        that's not really there
          when in *reality*
      we walk the line between
             called
           the shore.

Surfing

He said,
let's walk on moonlight
and be the distant strangers
those figures hope to know
      who stands alone
      unknown.

All at once
standing is being born
again,
and I brush the backdrop
      I've never seen
      convene.

The earth moves
underneath me, and
fog shatters like glass
from the hum
      my carving gait
      resonates.

The canvassed town
seems foreign now
as I approach with
regal tenderness
      from the crashing dynasty
      that sets me free.

Jetties

Be warned,
once you walk out
you never really come back.
And in the days
for the rest of your life
your body
is like the ocean
and other days
like the rocks.

Over time,
out of reach,
those rocks will be gone
embraced by the sand
that the sun won't remember
quickly enough.

They are the marriage
my grandparents had stolen,
my parents denied themselves,
and my children will believe in.
Steadfast,
beautiful,
together -

keeping the world
we know
from falling apart,
washing away,
and left in pieces
for the ignorant,
everywhere else,
to find and ask
what's this?

Rogers

I hit the bridge
and the crowd calls out.
In the right moment,
the sun shines my direction
through that familiar arch
of summer's castle.
Somewhere
I grew up
in the sea of footprints -
the passage
that smells of ancient fires
and shines like
the glittering ocean
in our hair.

This pavilion
is a rite,
and you know it.
It brings us together,
it's what we share.

It is the
          culture
that we bleed on to the
          canvas
as we paint the
          caves
we hide and explore in with the
          companion
who remembers everything.

Because with each breath
it breathes on the shore
it gives me its essence
and takes a little piece
of mine.

Seashells

In a wandering vexation
I came across two seashells
that were more than they appeared.

Although they looked the same,
both delicate and pure,
their serene hearts
revealed distinct voices
that whispered
with my ocean behind them.

They know all
I did once,
and the one thing
I can't think or say.
And I envy them
of course.

They are together
always
with no ocean or beach
large enough to say differently.

Each with its own
lovely pearl
that I had the pleasure
of knowing briefly
in my wanderings.

CONTEMPLATIONS

The Mind
An Early Poem

I find myself in a place
where my thoughts linger,
awaiting remembrance.

A place where my memories
meet and discourse,
where
my senses eavesdrop
silently
hidden in the diminishing shadow
of the unknown.

Ordinary Art

In the realm
of my imagination
she stands
against a storm of the mundane
and screams her voice dry
of the beauty she sees,
no,
believes is there.
Against all will of nature
and all prescribed fears
she howls!
and hopes to grasp
just a handful,
enough to show
a fool like me,
a boy like me,
who watches
this woman standing
on the tip of a needle
against the onslaught
of reality.

I have seen what happens
when an unstoppable force
meets an immoveable object
and it is no ordinary art,
my friends.
It is the place to start
it was a world apart.

The Imagination

Watch, you move as freely
as a queen
with thoughts preserved
in squares as bold
as night and day.

There's an inverted host
who welcomes
your way out
with a guiding hand
revealing all
but his shadow behind you.

But thankfully
this garden needs shade
to grow your castle,
your beast,
your faith.

What comes next
is no surprise,
only part of you hopes.

The Rain

When chaos restrains
and you're down on your knees
everything rains.

Emotions can't wane
despite all your pleas
when chaos restrains.

If you leave reason slain
to set your soul free
everything rains.

Nothing's left to regain
as you hoped it would be
when chaos restrains.

Just observe the mundane,
and then you will see
everything rains.

And though the world seems insane
just take it from me,
when chaos restrains
everything rains.

Silence

I imagine myself
sitting where I am
now
in the great kind of
solitude
that can only be imagined.
I ask myself,

> *Would I come back here*
> *alone?*
> *Would I sit here*
> *facing an empty world*
> *alone?*
> *Would I have the courage*
> *to travel far off*
> *and see things anew*
> *alone?*

I ask myself this
because I am
alone.

And solitude is
that empty cave
who protects you
from the elements
but swallows you whole
when you realize
you've gone on
too far.
Courage won't matter then
because animals don't have it.

Night

My mind
collapsed nicely
under dusk's eager fiend
and in the soft burning moonlight
I see
my fancy brooding inverted.
Blissful, nude desire
Oh, go easy
on me.

At last,
the unwanted
pleasure sanctuary
betrays under my allowance.
Ah, shit.
Look around you hopeless rookie.
You can't reach in the dark
all through the night.
Just go.

#40

Don't nod
for my life is
never odd or even.
Rest assured on the dreams that I
refer.

Refer
to the question nobody asks;
won't lovers revolt now?
Try not to stare.
Don't nod.

Ode to the Basement

I'll only stay an hour more
and lose myself beneath the rug
and travel further than the floor
within my heart no spade has dug.
You hold our den, no arms to bear
just eyes to gaze and teeth to grit
and dust collected on my bones.
Down here there's not a flaw to spare
besides the empty hollow pit
to stay once winds of age have blown.

The Band Room

Play on, play on eternal songs.
The walls ring out my whole life long.
We can't see past baton's decree
nor coda's call eloquently.
Deny sense of right and wrong.

The children laugh with hearts so strong,
and strangers come to play along
keep up, insist, follow our key
play on, play on.

Repeat it twice, our fates prolonged.
You'll find the melody belongs
with hand and bell upon your knee
finale not in spite to see
no halting soon and ere the gong
play on, play on!

303A

Inside room 303A is at least 21 years,
not counting the ones I imagined.

I remember the snow,
a curtain in the air,
lighter than my breath,
whispering a warning
of the promise between each flake.

And somewhere between the reeds
and the temple
I stumbled
over nothing
with bare feet moving forward
and closed eyes looking back.

Inside room 303A is some other fool now.

The Road of the Sun

I've hung around too long
listening to the old main street songs.
And I need to start down that road
'cause the sun's too heavy
for the clouds to hold.
And I don't really mind to go,
for when the darkness starts to grow
no one can predict my fate,
and I'll out run the traveling sun
leaving shadows in my wake.
My footsteps will burn in the fires of time,
and I'll just laugh with haste in my climb
because the darkness is heavy with emptiness
making it mine to fill with who knows what
a smile, a dance, my lips sealed shut.
I'll then emerge from a country of smoke
made of secret love with no whispers spoke.
And in that dawn you'll see my face
atop the noble ruins past
left crushed beneath my quaking pace.
I'll love the spoiled feels and sounds
and strike it first, the public drowned
with no vindication at first light
because if I want to change the world
I have every damn right.

THINGS GOLDEN

The House Above the Earth

Let's continue.
Going up
or going down
ain't so bad either.
Because the roads,
the stars,
the winds
all lead to the house above the earth
where every child wants to live
and play
and laugh.

Let's take off our clothes.
Wearing the sky
doesn't mean you can fly
but you don't have to walk
or run
or fancy
the house above the earth
where age takes second place
over a bronze dream.

Let's swim.
You know where,
ah, but you don't care
and who's to blame
when things aren't the same
or nice
despite
the fact remains
that all is left
is to find that place
where going in
is to coming out
to you know where.

The Eyebrow Conundrum

Sometimes an eyebrow
is just an eyebrow,
or in this case
a stormed hemisphere
striking a single bolt
or ray of sun.

The box
an ignored poet speaks atop.

A country
for a single dune.

A conundrum
revealing a shade of truth.

Or sometimes it's just an eyebrow
I see each morning,
wondering if I'm getting older
or just awesome.

Like

It whispered
like a soft rain
that I almost mocked.

There it was -
the glass house
I believed had secrets.

Then she came -
the lioness
greeting my wet idiocy.

I married her.

What Waits Around

The ground looks the same,
how lovely,
and your fear won't let you
see the world in the leaves
you cling to.
Don't find the center,
find a center.
The single path
is for the ignorant.
What waits around
can be better than
what waits within.
But that's for you to decide,
when those snakes
offer you a route.
How lovely.

Foxes & Owls

Says you,
the standard fox
who leaves in flights of fancy.
I've never seen you
until yesterday
when daylight was rescued
by a quieter hour.

Don't leave yet,
or am I just a signpost
towards an unnecessary path?

I can be your owl
perched on highest branch,
laughing at your level
with hidden wisdom
you know is
so sweet.

Smile Sounds

It isn't like
we're waiting for silence
with fingers crossed
above sweaty palms.
And the song
is never over,
because it hasn't started,
but keeps going on.

Untitled

It's that part of ourselves
that we hide away.
We hold that part of us
like a book beneath our sleeve
as we run home in the rain.
There's something in that
solitude
that I love,
and we're all too afraid
to speak of.

Whispers in the dark.

That's not enough,
and it's our fault.
We scream
for the world
just over the edge,
but when the lights
are off
no one panics.
We just take that part
of ourselves
out,
       hold it,
       and maybe apologize.

I'd rather race
the bleeding print
in the storm
than pretend
those raindrops
are my tears.

To Teach and to Delight

And now the savvy, but weary, traveler
is faced with three choices.

To lay in the grass
watching day and night bicker,
and wait silently
for the rain.

To roll off the earth,
dig deep for a spring,
and drink back the strength
needed to climb the way out.

To walk towards a river,
heard somewhere far off,
through deepening woods
across new frontiers.

Shame

Afterwards,
I always love those days.
It's beautiful out,
and I've made myself feel sick
with a faithful companion
that whispers
in my ear
that I am alive,
and this is
the only way
I can know for sure.

I can't appreciate it then,
but I try,
and I'm getting better
unfortunately.

Words

The world is wet,
and we don't have enough
strength left in our hands
to wring it out.
So I say,
let's soak.
Let's soak
in the words
that brought us here
until the river
peaks above the shore,
and our stomping grounds
become unfamiliar.
I'll sway
and soak
in the tide
as it sweats off
the world
through space and time.
Because the ends are fading,
and I'm forever stuck
in between
soaking.

Glory of the Snow

The Glory of the Snow
is such a sweet disease.
On these spring mornings,
afternoons,
and nights,
I walk fast enough,
and my world seems purple.

HEARTS & MINDS
Haikus

Dad Knows

My father's quaint words
bring humorous nostalgia
just as he wanted.

Wisdom in Sag Harbor

After it was done,
I found an old conch seashell
echoing times past.

Gleason Emptiness

The last has been drunk
and summer sun shines elsewhere;
that road was epic.

The Shelves, Oh the Shelves!

House of potations
I aged with your tenants and
the shelves, oh the shelves!

Somethings

What I didn't bring
was left behind anyway
in summer somethings.

Sidewalk Dance

The flowers and drunks
set the stage in August craze;
a dance I can't step.

The Tale of Dickey D.

This man was a drum
signaling the changes for
sweeter melodies.

The Funny Side of Tragedy

Let's gather and try
to be serious this time
in silly remorse.

Samantha

A story of strength -
a girl who did not fret and
stands above us all.

When You Have Them

With words sewn freely
their hearts and minds will follow
to the very end.

What Hasn't Been Said

For the distant ones,
something keeps us together
I know we cherish.

OUTSIDE PERFECTION

The All-Knowing

Suppose it's not
your run-of-the-mill
perfect world
where happiness is dropped
at the first chance of pity
and where the famed
resort to all kinds of
method violence.

Why not live
outside perfection,
for just a moment,
and burn in
the all-knowing
as you stand on the sun
and watch the earthrise.

Can you sweat it out
just long enough to say
you did it,
you saw it,
what's next?

Ethos

It's that feeling
that permeates my skin
like a lucid dream
I'm realizing
this very instant.
Basking in it
with liberal concentration
opens the windows
to let in the air
and the world breaths
a sigh of relief
knowing that I can feel it
and want to make
a change.

It's a feeling
outside perfection
that I've hidden away
seven times
so far.
Find them all
and you'll find part of me.

Amelia Pond

Go west
until you see
the lord written out
like fire on the mountainside.
Climb past the stars
where the lonely men dwell.
Through these trees I love
to a bridge incomplete;
a piece is left there.

The Hidden City Near Dusk

It lies just before tomorrow,
between my past and future.
I visit it often,
shrinking my feelings
to walk the streets
that flood with time.
A piece is left there.

The Tree That's Not for Real

This was the tree
that couldn't make up its mind.
And the storm finished the job for it,
intervening like a tried mother
who embarrassed even me.

It still blossoms
every now and then
when I think to remember it.
And so,
a piece is left there.

Atop Kirkland

This was the place
where our legacy was born,
where on late winter nights
no brick walls
behind glass doors
could contain me.
Where the square pathways
above this ringed road
weren't high enough
for me to dream of
tomorrows
to be spent elsewhere
and with you.
I found my way
off the top
but a piece was left there.

The Spire Unseen

A place I've never been
just seen from afar
or stood under
through youth
and youth
much wiser,
I'd like to think.
It seems only logical
atop these halls of first love,
where I learned of a broken heart
faster than the tests could save me,
that a piece be left there.

The Indecisive East

Oh how I'd love
to be swallowed
by this island.
I would course through
the indecisive east
under great waters
and everything
would grow out of me,
be born out of me,
live on through me.
There is a garden
in my mind
with room
for one more.
And it bleeds
a fragrance
like illumination.
We all face the choice
when heading east.
But don't pass off the notion
towards roads of tidal motion
and a view seen so rare
of the piece that's left there.

The Seventh One

It's the seventh one,
and that's where it's always been
and that's where it stays.

It's kept close at hand
watching the sunset while I
look out past the shore.

It's the seventh one
and that's where it's always been,
the piece that's left there.

Catharsis

That release
from fingers wrapped around your throat
you confused for a nemesis.
Now you know,
but next time won't be any easier.
And that's what makes you the fool.
What makes me the fool,
different from you though,
is all this.

Outside Perfection

There's something
about all of us
that some see
and most others ignore
that is outside perfection
and a little bit more.

Truth lies
in the beyond
that you left behind
for a sweeter deal
offered from stranger hands
with familiar appeal.

Don't wait
for anything
if all you want
is right now
from seeing in the dark
somehow.

SNARKY AESTHETICS

What Nice

I don't know why you
skip the best kind of something
that doesn't make sense.

The Importance of Cups

I see children in the past
stacking cups in play without thinking
because it's there and it matters.
And eventually that pyramid reaches its peak
         and this is when the road forks
when the children choose to continue on
and stack from the top, one on another,
and the whole shape of things change;
the pyramid reveals a column
growing weaker from the child's persistence
that's blinding him from the others
who returned to the already,
grew the foundation of cups,
the foundation of everything we know
and changes all we knew
and all we'll come to know
in an instant.

And already I dread the approach
of the figure bred from cruelty
who'll knock over those cups and move on.
And I'll come forward to the child,
who'll already be rebuilding, and say,
"that's the world we make, and you did it right."
Then the child will think and hopefully ask me,
"why did you just stand there?"
And I'll be shown as the fool
when I realize I wasn't dreading at all
but compliant with the child's demise
because now they know and it had to happen.

         It's not about finding the new frontier
         and relieving yourself of the flag
         you carried longer than you expected.
         It's about looking at the already
         and seeing it differently.

Christ in a Sidecar

Yesterday I went outside
and spent time in the future,
which was so nice.
I was the man in town
who the old ladies and out-of-work husbands
ran to for help
when the mad-dog came strutting up the street.
One-shot Doyle, they called me,
in the future.
That's the kind of modest glory
my future will hold.
And I'll surprise them all
when I race away across the plateau
with Christ in a sidecar,
against the desperately protesting wind
pushing us back from the approaching cliff.
And I smile when I hear him say
"We're gonna need a miracle…"

Panic in Argyle

I found myself standing knee deep
in a lake.
My friends were on the shore
throwing stones and laughing.
Their punch-lines were
crisscrossing in the water
in a pattern I was either growing out of
or melting in to.
Either way,
this was no good.

A Side of Bees
This happened

A hive of bees
is no place for me,
especially when one falls
through the open sun roof of your car
after you've decided to delay work
a few minutes longer to enjoy spring.
Still,
they seem disoriented enough
to wait until the end of this song
before another bad decision is made.

For the Weak and Weary

Hold your breath
for just a moment
and listen to that silence
at the back of your throat
that screams of emptiness
as wide as winter in the Catskills
and as still as two sleeping lovers
holding hands.
When you feel that silence move
just an inch
open your eyes and imagine
looking closely at yourself,
seeing that moment etched under you eyes.
Fall in love with the reality
that there is nothing you can do about that.

Argot

The criminals and teenagers
have a way of talk
that ties your stomach in knots
and opens the windows of your heart
to a cold dark outside world
that's changing.
Am I right?
I see you on the sidewalk
sneering that sneer
for the sake of sneers
everywhere.
You can't fool me,
no, no.
You grasp it more tightly
then any of us.
So tight,
you can taste it in your fingers
when you hide under old sheets and shame
at night while hoping for the wind
to catch the window again.
I pity the bird shot down
and stuffed into the pillow
you rest your pompous head on.
A bird that migrated, of course,
but was still more of a local
than you.

Railroad Deviants

On this side of the tracks
the world revolves around
the quarters we collect,
the carcass we presume transcended,
the man-made lake,
the bridge we built by hand,
the bridge the earth let fall,
the paths we've carved with time,
the graffiti we scoff
from lesser railroad deviants,
the conductor with his x and y business
that we prance upon.

Family

Three stags wandered through the forest.
Over time, the eldest befriended the crickets
and shared songs for them to sing
softly in the night.
The second came to the stream to drink
and met a heron, scribing on the surface
and they talked forever.
The youngest came to see the falcons above
and, in time, learned to fly himself.
These deer were strange.

The End

A sailor in a storm
looks out astern
and sees the rocks approaching.
Below is who-knows-what
and behind is no longer an option.
The sailor swigs once more
with real prayer it won't be his last
and then convinces himself
that the best thing about the end
is that it is never the end.

The Last Key

Once when I was a kid,
I sat beside my mother
as she was playing the piano.
In my mind I remember
looking at that last key -
A,
and how her hands never
made it down that far.
I reached for it,
for the end,
to contribute on the neglected key
and I fell.
There is a scar above my left eye
from when I visited the edge of the universe.

Special Thanks:

Kelsey Erwin
Terry Lucas
Katie Pearce
Kelly Russell

Made in the USA
Charleston, SC
08 July 2011